AN AWAKENING AT NAIN

By Robert Darrol Shanks Jr., PhD

Copyright © 2023 AN AWAKENING AT NAIN

Published by: Writers Publishing House
Printed in the United States

ISBN: 978-1-64873-412-0

All rights reserved. No part of this book may be reproduced in any manner whatsoever without written permission from the author except in the case of brief quotations embodied in critical articles and reviews

Unless otherwise indicated, Bible quotations are taken from New International Version (NIV) © 1995 by Zondervan Publishing House and New King James Version (NKJV) MacArthur Study Bible © 1997 by Thomas Nelson, Inc.

CONTENTS

TO THE READER..i

ACKNOWLEDGEMENTS v

INTRODUCTION vii

CHAPTER ONE: THE HEALING..1

CHAPTER TWO: BACK TO WORK......................................10

CHAPTER THREE: THE PERILOUS JOURNEY TO JERUSALEM...22

CHAPTER FOUR: FEARFUL TRAVEL RETURNING TO NAIN...28

CHAPTER FIVE: THE ROAD TO SYCHOR........................45

CHAPTER SIX: A REVELATION 48

CHAPTER SEVEN: THE IMAPCT OF CHRISTIANITY.......52

CONCLUSION 57

ABOUT THE AUTHOR 60

TO THE READER

The life of Jesus and all that He represents has always held a fascination to me from the time my railroad father Robert D. Shanks senior introduced me to what it meant to know our Savior Jesus Christ. While I have had all the trials and disappointments of life as we all do, I continually go to the Bible seeking out its guidance. The Bible has all the lessons of how to live life right at our fingertips to guide us even in this high technology world.

I always wondered what happened to those in the Bible after their healing encounters with Jesus. What were their lives like after they were healed or after they had finally accepted the fact that this was indeed the chosen son of God? *"This is my son, whom I have chosen; listen to him."* (Luke 9: 35) How did these changed individuals interact with their communities and families after they were healed? How did they change their attitudes about life? Did they start churches? How did they follow the teachings of Jesus in a troubled time under the occupation of Rome? Were they persecuted or did they become beacons of light? Just what happened to them? What happened to the Roman Centurion that had so much faith that his servant was healed without Jesus visiting his home, this instance prompted Jesus to be amazed at his faith. So many questions emerge as we read the Bible about those that were healed. There are no definitive answers about their daily lives after their healings except to know that through His redemption life and their futures are secured. There are so many healed and changed individuals, so many whose stories are not chronicled at all and often just barely mentioned, in phrases like "…and many were healed."

Our modern times have had healings and changes with those individuals going on to do the work of the Lord, some work is monumental, some is just simply being a disciple of Christ and witnessing quietly in their daily lives. Some individuals are destined by the Lord for great works and some for quiet works.

The glitz and glamour of our modern times can cloud ones understanding and historical perspective of Christianity. The media often seems to relegate Christianity as almost irrelevant in how it is used in news reports. There seems to be at times a minimization of evangelical belief as a major faith in God. The media has more-or-less propagandized the term evangelical to a level of unimportance. So just what is an evangelical? The definition of the word evangelical according to The National Association of Evangelicals, NAE/Life Way Research, includes these statements to which respondents must agree to be categorized as evangelical:

- *The Bible is the highest authority for what they believe.*
- *It is particularly important for me personally to encourage non-Christians to trust Jesus Christ as their Savior.*
- *Jesus Christ's death on the cross is the only sacrifice that could remove the penalty of my sin.*

Only those who trust in Jesus Christ alone as their Savior receive God's gift of eternal salvation.

Visit Online Website (nae.net/what-is-an-evangelical)

The term evangelical has become a label for a group of believers. One must be careful of how labels are often applied to groups of individuals in our society. Labels can be so easily misunderstood and misused. Historically speaking, our modern times are now experiencing a severe polarization. Does Bible prophesy predict this? This question and many more will arise and can be answered through faith and a deeper exploration of God's word the Bible.

Therefore, the purpose of this historically based fiction is to project what might have happened after the miraculous healing in Nain, how an individual living in that time could possibly have changed because of Jesus Christ's direct touch. What kind of impact did he or she make after Jesus touched and healed them? What kind of trials did they have to endure? How did job, family, and community change in reaction to the one healed? I am not a pastor. I am one who believes in Jesus Christ and His saving grace. Perhaps this story will help in your journey of faith and the connection to His atonement with our world today. We have Jesus Christ's direct touch through scripture, for He came to redeem all who will believe.

    Historically based fiction can help a reader gain some insight into a time long gone. As an example, the fictional novel Johnny Tremain is a work of historical fiction written in 1943 by Esther Forbes and is set in Boston during the American Revolution and provides readers with a glimpse of life during that time. Hopefully, this fictional short story will provide the reader a better insight into that Biblical time frame.

ACKNOWLEDGEMENTS

AN AWAKENING AT NAIN is a deeply individual experience of faith in trying to bring into focus my own journey in Christianity. I could not have done this without the backing of my wife and soul mate *Cindi LaSalle-Shanks*. She has stood by me in thick and thin in my moments of frustration and feelings of inadequacy to even attempt such a project. Her encouragement in my life is invaluable. She has been my proofreader and has suggested valuable changes.

Of course, my children are all so supportive, **Krystal Klueckman, Kurenia Barnes**, and **Bradley LaSalle**. Without such wonderful children, a father can lose sight of goals and objectives in life. This book is also for all my wonderful thirteen grandchildren and six great grandchildren who are a constant delight and source of amazement. I owe a big thank you to them for helping me keep an innocence of attitude, the wonderment of discovery, the addition of current ideas and the maintenance of a positive view of life through Christianity.

AN AWAKENING AT NAIN is dedicated to the memory of our four deceased children, *Robert Scott Shanks, Kandace Leigh Shanks-Tettleton, Steven Allan LaSalle,* and *Diana Lynn LaSalle-Hontz.*

INTRODUCTION

Our story starts in the New Testament in the book of Luke chapter 7 verses 11 - 17.

Jesus is coming into a small town called Nain and sees a dead man in a funeral procession and is impacted by his widowed mother's grief and heals the man bringing him back from death and giving him back to his mother.

The small town of Nain was located southeast of Nazareth (see map). Modern Naim (ancient Nain, Arabic Nien) is on the lower slope of Mount Moreh. In the middle of the village, overlooking Mount Tabor is the Nain church, built by Franciscans in 1880 on the site of an earlier Crusader church commemorating Jesus' miracle. Nain, probably is of Hebrew origin, has the meaning "beauty" is nestled on a plateau on the lower northwestern slopes of Mount Moreh, southeast of Nazareth. Also known as "Little Hermon," Mount Moreh rises 1,815 feet above sea level and is parallel to Mount Gilboa to the south. It was here in Old Testament times that Gideon and his army of three hundred, (some accounts say 32,000) armed with trumpets, torches, and swords, attacked, and routed a superior force of Midianites (Judges 7:125).

Medieval pilgrims mentioned a church at Nain that was later incorporated into a mosque. In 1181, the Franciscans built a modern chapel in the center of the town. Outside the village, to the west, are some tombs of a Roman necropolis (Greek, "city of the dead") or cemetery.

Visit online website
(welcometohosanna.com/LIFE_OF_JESUS/028_Ministry8Nain.htm)

This is the first of only three instances of Jesus raising someone from the dead, the others being Jairus's daughter and Lazarus. The Jewish custom of the time was for the individual to be buried was carried in an open coffin. According to the footnotes in the New International Version (NIV), to touch the dead was a ceremonially defiling act of Jewish customs but Jesus' power dispelled all the horror of death and defilement. The New King James footnotes as well as the NIV for this passage go on to say this bold act is further evidence of how impervious Jesus was to such customs and defilements of the time.

After this encounter and healing, nothing else is known about the young man. We don't know his name, or his age and we don't know his mother's name. We are left to wonder what Jesus had in store for this young man after his healing.

The study of the author Luke brings forth many interesting facts as further background to our story. Most writers agree that Luke was most likely a Gentile, a non-Jewish individual. He writes as a meticulous historian according to New King James Version (NKJ). He was well educated in Greek culture, a physician by profession, and a companion of Paul during some of his missionary journeys according to the New International Version of the Bible (NIV). His style is that of a scholarly, well-educated man. The introduction to the book of Luke in the NKJ Version points out that a running theme in his gospel is Jesus' compassion for Gentiles, Samaritans, women, children, tax collectors, sinners and others often regarded as outcasts in Israel. It appears his gospel is targeting a Gentile readership according to the New King James Version. According to the NIV, Luke had an outstanding command of the Greek language. His vocabulary is extensive and rich.

The New International Version (NIV) Bible indicates the book of Luke was probably written between A.D. 59 and A.D. 63. According to the NIV introduction to Luke, this Gospel was written to strengthen the faith of all believers and more importantly to show that the place of the Gentile Christian in God's kingdom is based on the teaching of Jesus. It is clear he wanted the gospel to go to the entire world, again according to the NIV introduction to Luke. The NIV also indicates that Luke was probably a Gentile by birth too but well educated in the Greek culture and a physician by profession.

One must understand the word "gentile" as used by Biblical translators. As used, it simply means all those not of the Jewish faith or non-Jew, but it can also mean "nation" or "race" and is largely misused and misunderstood. We all are "lost sheep" Jesus came to redeem. He is our Lord. We all are all of one race, humans, He came to save.

So, this short tale is only to whet your appetite for more understandings of Jesus and the transformation he brought to a fallen world.

Judaea, Idumaea, Galilee and Samaria During Jesus Time

Nain is southeast of Nazareth and southwest of the Sea of Galilee

(Nain is in the red box)

CHAPTER ONE:

THE HEALING

Soon afterward, Jesus went to a town called Nain, and his disciples and a large crowd went along with him. As he approached the town gate, a dead person was being carried out – the only son of his mother, and she was a widow. And a large crowd from the town was with her. When the Lord saw her, his heart went out to her and he said, "Don't cry."

Then he went up and touched the coffin, and those carrying it stood still. He said, "Young man, I say to you, get up!" The dead man sat up and began to talk, and Jesus gave him back to his mother.

They were all filled with awe and praised God. "A great prophet has appeared among us, "they said. "God has come to help his people." This news about Jesus spread throughout Judea and the surrounding country. **(Luke 7:11-17)**

My first realization was of being bandaged, wrapped tightly in something as I felt hands tearing at my tightly covered body's garments. Where was I? The warm sun streamed across my face, as my eyes were uncovered. I felt a strange sense of complete calm, a complete peace within that I had never known.

I sat up momentarily dazed and confused, I struggled to take off the covering from my face and then my eyes locked upon Jesus, I knew He was my healer and instantly I seemed to know all that He represented. I knew He was the son of God; He had healed me and yet I had a strange realization I had come from a place of total peace and beauty but couldn't completely remember just where I had been.

Though I was wrapped in cumbersome linen, I got up from the mat the processional mourners had hurriedly placed on the ground as the "dead man" began to sit up. They all stood back in shocked horror as they looked down upon me. But I wasn't dead!

I got up and embraced Jesus, He then gave me back to my mother, Leah, who sobbing with joy hugged and kissed me saying "Ethan, my Ethan." The crowd of mourners and processional continued to slowly fall back in fear not wanting to be ritually unclean by touching a dead person, but I wasn't dead! The crowd was still in a total state of awe; but my mother was in a state of complete joy.

Some in the crowd were praising God saying a great prophet has appeared but some held back not knowing what to believe. Some ran away spreading the news of my healing and restoration. Some said he was only temporarily sick, just in a deep sleep, others were wondering if this was a demon possession.

My memory of being sick was punctuated with a vague memory of a bright light and of being in a place of complete peace and tranquility but somehow, I just couldn't remember much, just being in my sick bed and then suddenly sitting up in the middle of a funeral procession. Was this really my funeral procession? What is going on here? I was confused as my mother gave me some water and bread. She was talking rapidly asking questions along with those not afraid of me about where I had been, what had I remembered, what I had seen? I was of little help. All I could remember and relate was this complete feeling of peace and well-being.

The look in Jesus' eyes was seared into my mind and soul as I had never known anyone with such piercing, eyes and yet, at the same time, a peaceful countenance. Jesus projected an all-knowing peacefulness and acceptance. He had an air of total understanding of everyone it seems. His total caring for others and of worship of His father God was something I had never seen before. My joy was unbridled, all I wanted to do was follow Him and witness to others of His grace, but I could see in His eyes and feel in my heart the quiet command for me to remain in Nain to work for Him here. Jesus and his followers moved on down the road, was this the last I would ever see of Him?

What was I to do? It seemed like just yesterday I was at work in the small carpenter shop my good friend and mentor, Uri, owned. Yet I knew I had been sick for a long time too.

As I ate and visited with my mother Leah, at home, she kept quizzing me, but I just didn't remember much, maybe later it would come flooding back, I was hopeful. She was so overjoyed she kept bringing me food and drink. Finally, I had to tell her I was quite all right and satisfied with her meal and to stop fixing more food. "Mother," I said, "this is quite enough food for now."

There was a knock on the door, as my mother opened it we were met with a huge smile on Uri's face, my employer, coworker, mentor, and friend. He embraced me tightly and asked me to come back to work soon, everyone there missed me. Uri also related to us that there were two factions in our small town of Nain that were in conflict over what had happened to me. One group felt I was called by God and was held in high esteem. The other group was spreading rumors that I was demon possessed and sent back by Satan to torment and mislead the town.

I had much to think about, but my first desire was to return to my carpentry work that I so loved. Uri agreed that the sooner I came back to work the better to quell all the rumors as everyone could then see I was again returning to my normal activities. But in my heart, I knew I had changed.

I wanted to know where Jesus was, where did He go? Why didn't He leave me any instructions? There were no answers to my questions. Uri said only that He and his disciples left shortly after my healing heading south to Jerusalem. I wanted so to talk with Him. I had so many unanswered questions. Somehow in my heart I knew that I was to stay in Nain; my work for Him was there. I was facing so many obstacles. How was I to deal with those unbelievers? What was I to say to those with so many questions? I could feel the rejection, the stand-off looks and wayward stares as if I was a strange being. I knew I must pray and go to the synagogue each day to ask for guidance from God. I must study His word more diligently and try to be an example for God and His son Jesus. Many did not believe He was God's son!

My next step was to get back to work, to try to find some normal pattern to my life. What is normal after this miraculous healing? I felt so good, no sickness, no symptoms of what I had been suffering and enduring for so long. I felt as if I was again a young man with so much energy. I missed the carpentry shop, the smell of wood and wood chips, the patterns of the cutting and assembly of projects. My mind reeled with the excitement of my good health.

I had to work and care for my mother so having the prospect of working again excited me as I loved working with wood. I tried to follow what news I could of Jesus whereabouts but couldn't get any firm information. I had heard once He was close to Nain but found out after He left the area. Twice I travelled to towns where He was reported to be staying but after arriving, I seemed to be late, and He had left. I could not venture far from Nain for the tradition of a son caring for his mother was an important responsibility. I hoped I would again be near enough to thank Jesus in person, I only hoped, and I prayed fervently the time would come soon that I could find Him and personally look upon His face and praise His love and caring for my healing.

Many in Nain felt I was not to be trusted, some felt I was indeed demon possessed. Many would not talk with me. The priests were constantly questioning me on the Sabbath and at worship times. Some of the clerics did not want to talk with me at all or even touch me and there was discussion among them I should not be allowed to pray or be in the synagogue. Thankfully, that was decided by the elders as not an option since most in the community had profound respect for my mother and my family. In my mind I thought, why deny a believer access to God's temple? I was thankful this was not considered further.

Even some of the children of our town seemed to back away from me while others, in their child-like acceptance of adults, treated me as normal. One small girl had asked her mother why I had a glow about my face and head. I looked at my reflection and all I could see was the same face as always but somehow there seemed to be a softer look in my eyes, my hair seemed even lighter at my temples! Oh no, was I aging prematurely due to all of this? My mother did say I seemed more at peace and had a calmness she had not noticed before.

I wanted to question that little girl further about this light or glow around my head that I and most others could not see but she and others could see, but how without alarming her parents. So, I decided not to ask her. What was this "light" around me she had seen? What did it mean? Why did some see it, and some did not and why do some children seem to see it and not adults? How was I to know who was seeing the glow and what was its purpose? Perhaps I would never know.

Who am I and why did this happen to me? My full name is not important, but my story is and perhaps it will help some to examine their lives and how they live. I am but a simple carpenter and perhaps that is why I was healed because Jesus too was a carpenter and lived a simple life.

CHAPTER TWO:

BACK TO WORK

Early the next day, I reported to work at my usual time and as I collected my tools I was immediately besieged by several friends and coworkers asking me the same questions my mother had asked. They seemed bewildered that I couldn't remember anything. But they just kept asking me as we strolled into the shop to begin work. Many of my close friends there all wanted me to touch them to heal their infirmities. Some had problems I was not even aware they had; it seemed suddenly I was not only seen as a healer, a physician but a counselor too! What was I to do? All I could say to my friends many requests, " I'm still sorting this all out, I don't know if I'm a healer." I'm still on the mend myself. I told them all to find out more about this Jesus, was He indeed the Messiah? Some at work believed in Him and some didn't, why was that?

    Uri met me at my work area and said, "Ethan how are you today?" All I could muster back was a grunt of bewilderment. Uri went on, "Don't worry Ethan, I have talked with everyone so just be your normal self." As I looked at Uri, I noticed he was examining my face closer than usual giving me an uncomfortable feeling and in his eyes was reflected those same questions surrounding the amazement of my miracle healing. I was thankful my good friend was standing with me even if he didn't have his questions answered and that he would be my companion in the quest to discover who I was now and what my new purpose in live was to be.

Work didn't seem much like it had been, of course I had missed many days over the last year due to my illness but I now had much more energy and positive outlook on life. There was the familiar smell of wood I had missed and the wood chips all over the floor and with workers scurrying to and fro working on projects. How would I now fit into this carpenter shop? Just as my thoughts were reeling the voice of Uri echoed across the shop floor, "Ethan, come here, we have the perfect project for you." Dazed, I shuffled across the floor wondering whether I would even remember how to work with wood. Carpentry is a rough, tough job at times, demanding a great deal of physical strength and endurance as well as great skill. So, I wondered if I had any skill or enough strength left after my illness and healing. I did seem to have a newfound self-confidence these days. I did feel strong and healthy for the first time in a long time.

Uri had taken a job for one of the local council members from the Sanhedrin, the Jewish high court. The council member, who worked for one of the Sanhedrin's high priests, wanted a box made of fine wood for jewelry and other family keepsakes. Uri knew I had made other superbly finished items for others coming to the shop wanting small chests and boxes. The job was to be a finely made decorative chest of olive wood, lined with cedar. The council member viewed me with a skeptical eye as I approached. He had heard of my miraculous return from the dead and wanted to meet me and seemed pleased I was the carpenter selected to fashion his chest. At least he did not ask me questions about my healing but simply told me how big he wanted the chest and what kind of carvings he wanted on the lid and was happy I could accommodate his wishes. He gave me a sketch of the figure he wanted to have the lid adorned with on its top. His directions were to have the box one Amot (cubit) square. (Roughly a 20-inch square chest)

Having such a prestigious job given to me made me a bit uneasy but also, I felt this would be ideal for me just to come back to work and keep my mind busy and off all that had happened to me. I loved to carve designs in wood and to construct finely fashioned benches and small tables, so I was delighted and began fashioning ideas in my mind and looking for suitable wood. It was good to be back at work and to smell the various woods and work with friends again.

I tried to find out as much news as I could about Jesus and where He was. Many travelers came through Nain, and many had news of Jesus, this wonderful prophet and what He had done and where He was. I once tried to see Him when some travelers had sighted Him in Nazareth close to our town, but He was soon gone from there when I arrived. I so wanted to talk with Him to find out about His work and to visit with His disciples. I consumed all I could about Him and what He was doing from travelers and others who had known Him, saw Him, and heard His sermons.

Rumor was that He was headed for Jerusalem but that was a long way from Nain, at least a 5- or 6-day trip and I couldn't be gone from my mother and work for that long. The trek was arduous through hilly roads and trails. Harsh weather was not the only hazard I could face going to Jerusalem. The heavily forested Palestine Valley of the Jordan River had lions and bears in the woods, and travelers often told stories of fending off wild boars. (Jerusalem is roughly ninety miles south of Nain)

Besides having to face wild animals there were bandits, thieves, and robbers (often called the night bandits) that lurked along the major trade route to Jerusalem. If I went, I would be a solitary traveler but perhaps I could join a trade caravan headed that way for protection. Traveling alone was not recommended. I did so want to talk with Jesus again and it looked like He was headed for Jerusalem.

Current information arrived as travelers passed through Nain; Jesus was indeed on His way to Jerusalem so I need to plan a trip there to meet Him and will discuss it with my mother and Uri at the wood shop. I know the trip is dangerous, but my father helped prepare me for this dangerous world by teaching me how to handle a sword and defend myself and fight despite the outrage voiced by some members in the Sanhedrin. My father told all of them, I wasn't being schooled in violence but in how to protect myself, something few of my peers experienced in their families now under Roman rule, especially to the extent I had been taught by my father. We nevertheless were devoted to our Jewish religion and beliefs. Learning to defend and fight could be mistaken by the Romans as a possible insurrection so Johnathan, my father, was cautious in his teaching me how to use a sword. I was also taught how to use the bow and arrow, not only for hunting but for protection as well. He constantly stressed using discretion, common sense and always being in a calm mind and to not provoke others or strangers.

    Our family was an anomaly in Jewish life especially because he taught me how to use a sword and to fight while others shunned learning to use a sword or other weapons to any degree. The many ancient wars and fighting in Israel's history had saddened many in the population. Despite those anti-war feelings and hate of the Roman rule my father wanted me to know how to protect myself. He had a curved Assyrian copper sickle sword but fashioned a new sword in his forge with a straight double-edged blade made of a strange metal, one of his treasured creations since that material with iron in it was difficult to work with and forge or even to obtain. He even made a round shield of leather stretched over a wooden frame; of course, these were now mine. I took care of the shield by keeping the leather oiled. This longer sword made of metals from the Far East taught to my father by a friend who had traveled there was a rarity to have in Israel, but my father was a talented iron and metal worker. My father never documented how he made this sword; it was so sharp and much harder than many of the bronze, copper and iron type short swords of the day used by the Romans called a Gladius sword. The blade on my sword had a keen shine and looked smooth, sharp, and glistened brightly in the sunlight. Ethan kept it hidden away, a very prized possession he didn't want others to know even existed. He was a very private family-oriented person. My father's brother and family didn't even know of this special sword he had forged and was now mine.

Even though we tragically lost our father to illness when I was only 14 years old, my mother was always there for me even though growing up in a single parent home was difficult and not looked upon favorably. Thankfully, my father's brother Mathias supported us and his family the best he could until I could support her. My mother Leah always made me feel I was normal and just like all the other children in our small village. My aunt Joanna, Mathias' wife and my mother's sister treated me like I was their child too.

Since I had no father to teach me a trade my uncle Mathias, a carpenter in Nain, took me into his care for training me vocationally. I wanted to be more of a metal worker as my father was, but he and my father often worked together as carpenters. Only my mother and I knew about the special sword my father had left me, not even my father's brother Mathias was aware of this long sword and that was how I wanted it to remain. The Romans had such tight controls on metal workers and few in Israel did this type of work and were often under Roman suspicion so the less information in families and communities, the better. The Romans would quickly seize any weapons and especially this highly crafted sword if they knew it existed.

My mother's sister, Joanna, was also an enormous influence keeping us all together as one large family. Because of all these loving family members I indeed had a future. I was really the only support my mother had outside of what little her sister could do for her. She had already lost me once and now I wanted to take a dangerous trip to Jerusalem and leave her again for this journey? She was adamantly opposed to such a trip.

I had to convince my mother to let me leave and travel to Jerusalem to see if I could meet with and talk to Jesus. Why did He heal me? What was I to do now? This would be a formidable task as I was her only support. She knew I could defend myself but would be against my traveling that far, she had almost lost me once. I would try to be a part of a larger trade caravan moving south to Jerusalem. Many of these trade caravans often had Roman soldiers for protection but many did not. Either way if I go at all, I will have to be careful.

I had to find the right time to approach Uri. He would not want me to leave the shop. I would have to finish or be close to finishing the many jobs he has assigned to me. The 90-mile trip to Jerusalem would be at least 4 days and another 4 days back. I would only be gone for the better part of two weeks; certainly, he could survive without me in the shop for that long!

My mother was quite resistant but as I explained my need to meet Jesus in person to thank Him and to talk with Him; she reluctantly agreed I should make the trip. Uncle Mathias was equally concerned about me leaving but understood why; he also was captivated by Jesus and his teachings.

I finally decided the best time to approach Uri was when the council member came to pick up his wooden chest, if he was well-pleased with my work; this would be the time to approach Uri with my request. If the council member was not pleased, I would not dare ask for any time off or other privileges. I probably would never meet Jesus again, my heart sank at these thoughts but there was a glimmer of hope in my mind, somehow, I knew I would get to see Him in person, I just seemed to know.

When the council member picked up his chest, he was delighted with how it turned out and wanted to talk with me. He gave me an extra bonus for my work. The generous bonus would support my mother while I was gone. This was a perfect time to approach Uri. I wasted no time in asking after the council member left. He was reluctant but agreed to let me go as he knew how much I wanted to meet Jesus, so he gave in and even wanted to help me with suggestions. He was aware of my weapons and training so cautioned me about appearing too much like an insurgent, a zealot or militaristic in my demeanor or appearance. He agreed I should be armed with at least a common sickle sword carried by many on their travels. Uri knew nothing about my prized sword. I knew I would take the longer sword but would keep it out of sight unless I needed it.

He assisted me in getting accepted as part of a caravan just as I had hoped, headed toward Jerusalem. This caravan was to be escorted by a small contingent of Roman soldiers. The caravan leader thought I was going to Jerusalem for Uri. The caravan leader was a gruff man and demanded all individuals follow his instructions. He was a long-time friend of Uri's, so he treated me calmly but also rather indifferently.

The small group of Roman soldiers ensuring our safety on the trip was a Contubernium, the smallest organized unit of soldiers in the Roman Army (usually eight legionaries), all armed and highly trained. The Decanus, or squad leader, was all business and tolerated little banter expecting everyone in the caravan to follow his orders. I discovered that most caravans could have over one hundred pack animals, but since ours was small, we only had twenty-five donkeys and just a few horses. Of course, the Roman soldiers guarding us all had magnificent steeds.

The trip to Jerusalem could be a treacherous 90-mile trek, with wild animals and the ever present "night robbers". However, with such a formidable looking group of armor clad and armed Roman legionaries as our escort we should be safe. I decided to keep my long sword well-hidden on my pack animal amid all my gear and worked hard at just looking like a regular Israeli working for Uri and going to Jerusalem for him who had set up this trip. At home and work I sometimes get strange looks and was often stared at due to the strange glow and light about my face. I will concentrate on keeping my face and head covered as much as I can during the trip since I never know who can see whatever this mysterious glow is about my face. I hoped no one approached me to ask about my appearance for I really don't know what my response should be.

The night before our departure was a sad one as my mother continually lamented about my trip and the many dangers we could face. She felt a little better when she understood the Roman contingent of soldiers was going with us both ways. Uri had done an excellent job of setting up and preparing for the trip. He also gave me some advice to follow, he said to keep silent and do what was asked and not draw any undue attention to myself. Of course, Uri did not know about the sword my father had given me or the training he had given me. If I am not careful, all this could flood me with a lot of unexpected and unwanted attention.

CHAPTER THREE:

THE PERILOUS JOURNEY TO JERUSALEM

The day of Ethan's departure dawned bright as he awoke early and began assembling his gear for the long trip to Jerusalem. He had already met all the individuals in the caravan and saw the Roman legionaries packed up and ready to go. The Roman soldiers were made up of a Contubernium called a tent group usually made up of eight men. That was exactly how many Roman soldiers, eight men, who were assigned to protect this caravan. This caravan consisted of eighteen travelers.

Most of the travelers were individuals on trips for businesses of some kind and seemed wary of each other and especially of the Roman soldiers. Ethan wanted to travel as light as possible to not attract any undue attention and to not be a bother to the caravan leader. His sickle sword was fastened to his waist and carried visibly; the worn leather sheath's outline clearly identified his weapon for all to see. Ethan's prized long sword was wrapped in a blanket and appeared to be just another bundled blanket for camping and sleeping for the long trip and would keep it well concealed in all his gear. The sword was easy to quickly unwrap in case it was needed in the event of hostilities along the road.

There were few donkeys in this caravan so most of the travelers carried what they could. The caravan leader had several highly admired horses at his disposal and was taking three on this trip for his personal use. Ethan's supplies were atop a small donkey near the end of the caravan where he would walk. Being near the end of the short caravan, Ethan could clearly see what was transpiring ahead as the caravan moved slowly on its trek toward the holy city.

Ethan's mind often was racing with thoughts of where Jesus might be in Jerusalem and what He was doing. He often thought of what he should say when he finally met Him. He had a fitful sleep as his mind raced in anticipation of this trip he had longed to take and hopefully finally meet Jesus of Nazareth.

I finally awoke at about dawn to the sound of the travelers beginning to stir and wake up to the sun as it was finally breaking the horizon. The Roman soldiers had already been awake and were silently gathering in a small group for a short breakfast. The gruff Centurion leader was silently pointing out directions as the soldiers scurried back and forth. The other travelers, some finally awake, were slowly getting up. There was no formal breakfast, it seemed everyone knew what to do and were breaking out their meager morning rations as they assembled their gear for the trip.

The trip was uneventful but on the last night of the trip I was awakened by shouting. The small caravan was under attack by a band of road bandits. In the dim campfire light, I broke out my long sword and between me and the Roman soldiers, the band of thieves quickly retreated with several wounded. My long very sharp sword was devastating but also not readily visible during the mele since it was dark and just before dawn. The Romans were impressed by the fact I was able to fight with such skill, especially the Centurion in charge as he eyed me with suspicion. I quickly put my prized sword away for fear it would be seized by the Romans should they had seen it and kept my short traditional sickle sword out. The Centurion leader asked me where I had learned to fight with such skill, all I said was I was trained by my father in self-defense. He seemed impressed but also highly skeptical of why I had such skills since I was Jewish. I continued to keep to myself. Some of the others in the caravan doubted I was really a Jew and wondered aloud who I really was and openly kept away from me as well. The Roman Centurion used his Sickle Sword well but that sword in reality was nothing compared to my long European sword made of the strange metal not readily available in Israel. My father's method of making this prized sword was not known in Israel and made it something that could get me into a lot of trouble and imprisoned or worse. I had to be careful in the future and would have to work at keeping my prized possession well hidden.

Coming into Jerusalem, it seemed there was a festival, a celebration of sorts, with loud raucous crowds drinking wine and in a party mode. The Romans were brutal in their occupation and tolerated little from the Jewish population. There was a crucifixion underway at Golgotha. There were supposedly three being put to death. As I came upon the hill, I was shocked to see Jesus of Nazareth was one of those being brutally put to death. What had He done? Why was this happening? I was devastated, He was said to be such a gentle individual and I had read and heard He openly cared about many of the downtrodden and the sick and especially about children.

No one could give me a rational answer for Jesus' crucifixion, only that He was betrayed by one of His own disciples to the brutal Romans and the hard and uncompromising Pontius Pilot, the regional Roman governor. I arrived just in time to see His death after hanging on the cross for over six hours. I was in total shock; I was in complete disbelief and unable to grasp the horror of seeing this slowly taking place before my eyes.

I was in Jerusalem for less than a day but had seen enough, I must leave and return to the safety of my home in Nain. It seemed everyone in Jerusalem appeared to not care and were there just to view the barbaric Roman method of justice, crucifixion. I still had no answers why Jesus was one of the crucified.

CHAPTER FOUR:

FEARFUL TRAVEL RETURNING TO NAIN

The horror of seeing this senseless crucifixion was something I could not endure, the only reason I came was to seek out Jesus and find out as much as I could about Him and thank Him in person for my healing. Now all I could do was hastily gather my possessions and look for another caravan heading north toward my home in Nain. I was in such a state of complete depression. Several of the same group of travelers were again on the road heading toward my home, so I joined them again and was surprised when the gruff Centurion leader was also again in charge of this caravan as he was tasked with protecting this group. All of this had been set up by my employer Uri, he carried more weight and influence than I realized. The Centurion seemed calm and a little indifferent when he saw me, however, he was still a rather harsh no nonsense Roman officer but why was he so suddenly relaxed around me? Did he somehow now see the glow or light around me some say they see about me face but others don't see? I was again full of more troubling questions, but the fact the Centurion was now more relaxed as he approached me was nothing short of a personal amazement for me. Perhaps he was glad I was on the return trip in case we were attacked by roaming road bandits again. He was quite surprised at my ability to handle myself with a weapon, something many did not know my father had taught me.

I wanted to question the Centurion about what he knew of Jesus' crucifixion, but thought better of it, perhaps later in the trip I would find a more private moment to talk to him, he was not a very approachable Roman officer. I was full of questions about the whole affair, the seemingly rush to judgment and "sham" trial of Jesus under Pontius Pilot. I had to be careful in my search for more information, I was already viewed with skepticism by many of the other caravan travelers who remembered me, many suspected I was not Jewish at all especially since I knew how to use a sword in a fight.

I did discover the Centurion's name, Atticus, I saw it scrawled on the back side of his leather belt he wore and where he carried his sheathed dagger. He also expertly wielded the twenty-eight-inch Roman Gladius battle sword also kept on his belt. He bore scars of past battles on his face and arms; he indeed was a large physical force to be reckoned with and was to be spoken to with deep respect at all times and only when necessary. My prized sword I kept out of sight was longer at thirty-four-inches but also light and easy to hold and seemed to me just as easy to use as his shorter Gladius sword.

As the travelers settled into various groups after the first day's travel, Atticus was tending to his horse so while I unloaded my pack mule, I asked him what he knew of the

Roman crucifixion of Jesus. I felt my question would be ignored so his candid response to me was a surprise. He stopped what he was doing and looked me straight into my eyes. He said what was so troubling to him was the reaction from one of the Roman officers he knew well and had served with. According to Atticus this individual was an experienced veteran officer of many conflicts and was held in high esteem by all the Roman soldiers. He related that just before Jesus' death he and Jesus locked eyes momentarily. The officer was almost incoherent in his response and resulting reactions. He related that Jesus' eyes were so penetrating as if He was looking deep into his soul and inner being. The veteran officer's reactions were so surprising, he related that he felt Jesus knew everything about him and could not understand the deep-seated peace he saw in His eyes despite the pain He was enduring. He had never seen anyone react like this while being so physically abused at a crucifixion, the officer felt such unexplainable and sudden unbridled shame at what he was doing to an obviously innocent man that no one in the Jewish crowd came forward to defend. Why would such a hardened combat veteran suddenly experience such remorse and shame?

    There was one new traveler on this homeward bound trip, a quiet but nervous individual named Aaron who quietly told some of the other travelers he was a new disciple of Jesus and was distraught at what had happened to Him and felt he had to leave Jerusalem as it was not safe for those who followed Jesus. I approached him but he, like many of the others, was not very forthcoming with me even though I told him of my admiration of what I had heard of Jesus. I hoped to tell him of my miraculous healing, but he didn't like talking with me. Perhaps I can talk with him more later since the trip home is five days, I will find a way to talk with him.

The third night of the trip started out as uneventful as the first and second days of the trip. Everyone settled down for the night but just after the sun had set the entire group fell under a fierce attack again from roaming road bandits. I again used my sword to fight off many of the attackers. I know I wounded one and saw the others scatter after my defense. I also noticed two attackers going after Atticus, so I jumped into the fight. The attackers seemed surprised that a simple Israeli could fight and wield a sword so expertly and immediately backed off, one was severely wounded and quickly escaped into the night bleeding from his wounds. This attack didn't last long. The Centurion Atticus was grateful for the assistance and gave me a nod of gratitude as the other invaders scattered into the night. I again quickly put my sword out of sight wrapped up and on my pack animal. We attended to our wounded as Atticus posted two Roman soldiers as sentries for the evening. I was now quite concerned for my sword, many questions raced through my mind, "How could I protect it now that it had been seen?" "Who in the caravan saw my sword?" "Could I continue to conceal it on one of the many pack animals?" "What should I say when

asked about it?" I had to stop this nervous worry and futile speculation about what might happen and just pray about the situation and go about my business as usual.

The next morning the Centurion sought me out quietly and away from the others as he had seen my unusual sword, it was not like the traditional Gladius battle swords his troops wielded. I knew he was curious about the sword, I feared it would be confiscated by him, but it was not. He had many questions about it as I related how it was made by my father and was a family heirloom. Nothing else was said about it but he did say to keep it out of view as it could be taken. I again was surprised at his not exerting his authority by confiscating my weapon. I had a deep feeling in my heart and mind that the Lord was with me and looking out after all of us in the caravan. Perhaps the Lord was directing the Centurion to his own salvation paths.

Since the Roman Centurion is now more open to me as he disciplines and oversees the caravan, I can feel it and see it in his eyes but I'm sure the other travelers haven't noticed that as yet. Perhaps I can explore what he knows about the crucifixion of Jesus. Did he know the soldiers there? What did he know of Jesus? What was the state of the Roman troops stationed in Jerusalem and what were their feelings about Jerusalem and the disciples? What kind of threat did Jesus really pose to Rome? It all seemed so strange and now far away and not at all real in my mind. I had so many unresolved questions and feelings, but I also knew I had to be extremely careful about when and how I voiced these concerns when approaching the Centurion. The last thing I wanted was to cause a rift and further shut down any information I might gain from the Centurion Atticus. And in the process, I might lose the prized sword my father had so secretly and wonderfully crafted.

As we moved into the fourth day of the trip, the countryside was calm with travelers and residents going about their business as usual. We were moving through areas with lots of brush and trees, it was suddenly becoming quiet with few people and activities. As we rounded a slight bend in the road near the town of Sychor, a band of five well-armed bandits suddenly came out of the bush and attacked us. Many of the eighteen members of the caravan were not armed or poorly armed and seemed to know little about how to defend themselves. Many were in a state of panic and shock. The Roman Contubernium and tent group of eight soldiers assigned for protection under the Centurion were well trained and disciplined. Even with this Roman protection the caravan again had to endure a second attack from road bandits. The group of eight Roman soldiers took up the fight quickly fashioning a rough circle around the hapless caravan travelers. I quickly found my prized sword, unwrapped it, and jumped into the fight!

Three of the road bandits seemed alarmed that a simple traveler would even fight or know how to defend themselves. They were astonished that I had this strange long sword and could use it well, they no doubt wondered where it had come from and why did this individual know how to use it so expertly? They meekly began to fall back quickly while two of the other seemingly well-trained bandits had joined the two fighting the Centurion Atticus. Atticus was a large Roman soldier and well trained and was defending himself well until two of the three bandits that fell back from the main fight moved into take out the Centurion. Now Atticus had four bandits slashing and attacking him. They knew taking out the leader would completely put the remaining Roman soldiers at risk and make overtaking the caravan much easier. However, they were wrong and severely misjudged the situation.

Atticus, seeing Ethan moving to help him with the fight seemed to energize him as he and Ethan expertly fought off the four attackers gallantly and quite professionally. The fight didn't last long, as the bandits could see the Romans were well trained and ready for them and to then have one of the seemingly weak caravan travelers suddenly begin to fight, really seemed to unnerve them and they quickly fell back into the brush to disappear.

Some of the eight Roman soldiers had slight injuries but no one was seriously hurt. Some of the travelers had huddled together in the midst of four of the Roman soldiers who bravely protected them, their goods, and animals. They were extremely shaken by the events since they were still only about halfway to Nain and still had a long arduous trip ahead.

Slowly the members of the caravan and soldiers began to reassemble the group and get it reorganized again so they could proceed. They had lost valuable time on the road but needed to get everyone back in line and ready to move again, this took some time. The animals had to be attended to for possible injuries, calmed down, fed, and watered and the supplies repacked so they could proceed after the sudden attack.

As the caravan got itself back together and reorganized, Atticus made a point to seek out Ethan and to thank him for his quick thinking and ability to rise to the occasion and thwart the sudden attack by the road bandits. He again didn't mention Ethan's sword but was grateful for the assistance since all his soldiers had their hands full fighting off the attackers. He seemed to know that the sword was safely back on the pack animal Ethan was using but made no mention of it. Some of the caravan members seemed to wonder how Ethan was able to assist and fight when most of them had scattered and were hiding in the brush and trees along the road. Some members thought Ethan had gotten hold of one of the road bandit's weapons and was using that to help beat off the invaders. When asked about that Ethan only shrugged his shoulders and said very little. He indeed was becoming something of a mystery member of the caravan headed toward Nain, his home. That evening as the caravan began to make camp, the Centurion had posted all of his men and they were all alert as well as assisting some of the caravan travelers.

  Quietly Ethan asked the Centurion what he knew of the man Jesus who was crucified. Atticus said he knew one of the soldiers who was assigned to Golgotha where the crucifixions took place. He related how this battle-hardened officer was grief stricken after being a part of those assigned to Jerusalem.

  He said the officer was visibly shaken by what had transpired, something he rarely saw since all the soldiers were highly trained in combat and had seen all kinds of fighting and brutality in various other Roman outposts. What bothered him was what Jesus had said just before dying, *"Father forgive them for they know not what they do."* That officer was strangely affected and didn't understand why this man was being crucified when He seemed so at peace. To whom indeed was he talking? All of the stories he had heard about this man did not fit what was happening to him and the verdict that Pontius Pilot had rendered. To see a fellow officer this affected by what was seemingly a regular and pointless sacrificial death that occurred often in that area was puzzling to Atticus. Although Atticus did again relate that Jesus eyes had such an unexpected penetrating effect on his friend. Atticus' comrade later said it felt like he was looking into my inner being and knew everything about him, something he had not expected. He really wondered who was this simple man, living and traveling in Israel? Atticus apparently had not related any of this information to anyone else and it was troubling to him why his friend was so affected. I was astonished he had even told me this at all. Atticus said his comrade's name was Marcellus, Atticus couldn't understand why his friend Marcellus was so fraught with a confusing regret he began acting completely out of character as a highly trained Roman officer, so much so, the Roman command was considering removing him from service, something that rarely happened. I could see this was quite troubling to Atticus to see a friend so fraught with uncertainty, regret, and confusion. I sensed Atticus wanted to question me more about this man called Jesus and what I knew of him. Did I even dare consider telling him what had happened to me? I thought better of it for the time being because I didn't really understand what had happened to me and why.

My training and use of my prized sword had seemingly opened an avenue for a level of communication not often seen between Romans and an occupied populace. Some of the caravan travelers were getting highly suspicious of me now and the fact that the Roman Centurion would even talk with me at all was a bit shocking to many of them.

I just couldn't keep my mind off my long sword. I wondered what lay in the future for me! Would I have to continue hiding my talents, one who was trained in the art of combat and swordsmanship, or would I be open and unafraid of anyone who knew of my skills?

Atticus was now quite relaxed around me and spoke easily with me about many Roman subjects and views of the current world. He often seemed to treat me as if I was a Roman citizen.

The long trek toward home seemed to be going so slowly. I was bone-tired at the end of each day keeping such a sharp vigilant lookout for more roaming bandits as we moved along the road.

The subject of metallurgy kept coming up about how my father had crafted this sword using some relatively unknown mixtures of iron and copper making it so much sharper and more devastating than the traditional iron or copper sickle swords. All I could relate to Atticus was many travelers had brought back strange products and methods of metal uses from India and my father, already good at working with metal, took in all the information and often experimented with these current ideas. While Atticus was more open and friendly, I still feared for the loss of my sword by him or possibly by what other caravan members knew and said to others about my fighting skills with this strange sword. What would Atticus say to his leadership when he reported back to his Contubernium of fighters and what information would be passed on to the higher echelons of the Roman Legion? All I could do was to plan how to escape and evade discovery and or eventual capture where I eventually could lose my prized weapon crafted by my father.

Many travelers would not interact with our group when seeing Atticus and his imposing group of eight soldiers. So, we had limited contact with news events. News often traveled quickly by word of mouth as peddlers, traders and others used the road to and from Jerusalem but seeing the armed Roman contingent escorting our group kept us from getting very much current news from the local populace. We were unaware of any Roman developments and relied on the Roman officers for information if they would even tell us anything.

While Atticus still didn't understand what these Christians were doing, he wanted to know more since his friend was so affected. He had to be careful not to show an interest in this religion but had more questions the more he found out about them. What really happened to Jesus' body after his crucifixion? He heard the body was stolen but those who worshiped Him said He rose from the dead after three days; what kind of power did this Jesus have over those who believed in Him? Atticus had many more questions than answers.

The quiet traveler Aaron approached me having heard from one of the travelers that I had been healed by Jesus. He now seemed to want to talk with me despite my friendliness with Atticus. He wanted to know about my miraculous healing. I told him all that I could remember. He also wanted to know more about my skill with the long sword and why it was so different than the swords commonly carried by the Roman centurions. I didn't tell him much, only that it was a family heirloom. Again, more to be concerned and worried for my prized gift made for me by my earthly father. I had to work to keep my faith in God strong and keep moving toward home. But would it be any better there? Perhaps just keeping the sword well-hidden at home would be enough. Aaron's interest in my sword indicated others in the caravan may have also noticed this unusual weapon and have questions as well. I needed to stay calm and focused.

As Aaron told me about himself, I was surprised to learn he was indeed a new disciple of Christ, a new believer and wanted to learn more about Jesus and His calm and seemingly unlimited love and knowledge of people. Aaron just didn't feel safe after the crucifixion of Jesus and the Roman treatment of Christians.

He decided to flee Jerusalem and because he had no family there, he really didn't know where to go, so he picked up the caravan headed for Nain. Aaron also related he really wanted to learn how to get more involved in serving Christ. He was so impressed with Him and His disciples. Aaron also said he was very worried at what possibly may have become of Jesus' disciples under such brutal Roman control. All we could do was to keep moving toward Nain with our guards up. Nain would be much safer as it is in the Center of the Samarian plain just south of Nazareth near Mt. Tabor. The concentration of Roman troops lay far to the south toward Judea and Jerusalem.

Because I had asked Atticus about what he knew of the crucifixion he shared with me the news that Jesus' body was gone from the tomb, a courier passing to the south told him of the rumor his body was supposedly stolen by the disciples of Christ. Another development hard for me to understand and even believe. Why was Jesus such a threat to the chief priests? The populace believed a Messiah was coming, was Jesus that individual? I have so many questions.

As we got nearer to Nain the number in our group began to dwindle as travelers going elsewhere left the caravan for other destinations. Aaron also left the caravan headed in a different direction than where we were headed.

A Roman courier arrived carrying orders for Atticus to return to Jerusalem so now our protectors would be marching back toward their Roman station in the south leaving what remained of the caravan to defend themselves. Atticus sought me out before turning his small force of Roman soldiers to the south. He confidentially told me to protect my sword and use it only when rare occasions arose. I was appreciative of his frank candor and the fact he did not seize my family weapon. Why he did not confiscate my sword was still a mystery to me but very much appreciated. In my heart, I felt a strange kinship with him, possibly because of our joint endeavors and battles to protect our small group of travelers. I would keep him in my daily prayers. I often wonder just what happened to him, did he retire to Rome at the end of his service? Perhaps I would never know. Our small group that was left watched as Atticus and his soldiers now turned and headed south leaving five of us alone now on the road to Nain.

CHAPTER FIVE:

THE ROAD TO SYCHOR

We were now on the road to the small village of Sychor as our small group slowly trekked north. As we arrived at the town of Sychor, the caravan continued to dissolve as travelers departed on different paths at Sychor. My beloved Nain is situated just to the north under Mt.Tabor and soon I would be close to home. In my mind, I can see my mother scurrying about and no doubt frantic for news from Jerusalem in the south. She will be overjoyed to see me return sooner than she had imagined.

My mind was made up to stay in Nain and help to spread the word of Christ and to relate what I had seen. I was so troubled that Jesus' body had been stolen from the tomb, why and for what reason? The rumor was Jesus' disciples took the body away. How did that happen as the tomb was guarded by Roman soldiers?

Our caravan now consisted of only three travelers, just me and a man named Cleopas and a man named Levi who would be delivering the goods my employer Uri had ordered from Jerusalem. The caravan leader rushed ahead to deliver the goods Uri had ordered. I would still have some time to spend with my mother before returning to work. I told Cleopas about my miraculous healing and all I wanted to do was to personally see Jesus and to learn what I could and to understand why I was healed but was unable to accomplish meeting Jesus. We encountered another traveler heading south who knew nothing of the events in Jerusalem. He chose to rest and talk with us before traveling south to Jerusalem.

Historical research has indicated the country of Israel was once more heavily forested with natural reserves of pine and oak trees all the way into the 19th century. In our modern automotive oriented society of today, many of our communities almost worldwide are linked with ribbons of asphalt and concrete roads. The development of electrical power and our many forms of instantaneous communication of course did not exist in Biblical times. Communication by letters was often slow and laborious. Additional historical research has estimated that at least 90 percent of the Jewish population of Roman Palestine in the first century could only sign their name or not write or read at all. The literacy rate was estimated to be about 3 percent.

Travel during Biblical times, even short distances, required extensive preparation and planning and could be dangerous for a lot of reasons. We take for granted our many modern conveniences and educational levels that did not exist in the time of Jesus.

CHAPTER SIX:

A REVELATION

The stranger wanted to know what we were discussing, Cleopas was amazed and asked if the person was a visitor to Jerusalem and why he was unaware of what had happened there in recent days. (Luke 24) We both were downcast and sad as we related the story about Jesus. We told him He was a great prophet, but the high priests handed him over to Pilot to be crucified for confusing and unknown reasons. We both had hoped He was the one who would indeed redeem Israel. I explained He had healed me, brought me back from the land of the dead and all I wanted to do was to talk with Him and thank Him and find out more about Him and His ministry, but He was gone as He and His apostles moved down the road soon after He had given me back to my mother. All of my past ailments were gone as well, I felt so renewed and alive. I made plans to go to Jerusalem when I heard He was now there to search for Him to thank Him personally, but I arrived too late, He had been crucified dead and buried. His body, according to the Romans, had been stolen from the tomb and rumors swirled about that He had risen.

Some of the women in his group of disciples went to the tomb where they had seen a vision of angels who said He had indeed risen. Many of His companions visited the tomb and He was not there. This was all so confusing to us and caused us great pain and sadness in our hearts. This stranger was indeed quite aware of what the scriptures and prophets had said about Jesus, so we were amazed He seemed to not know of the events that had transpired there. He was quite well versed in all the scriptures, He seemed to know a lot about Jesus. He told us nothing about himself as we slowly moved along the road.

Levi had already moved on ahead with several of his pack animals hurriedly heading for Nain to deliver the goods my employer Uri had ordered.

As they reached a small village, the stranger was going on, but we convinced him to stay with us as evening was approaching. (Luke 24) He decided to stay and have an evening meal. The stranger seemed to know much of what the prophets had said about Jesus and said we shouldn't be slow of heart that all of this had been foretold. How did this stranger seem to know so much about Jesus? As we sat and broke bread the stranger's appearance suddenly changed, we were astonished, He was indeed the Jesus and had risen, why hadn't we recognized him? As we sat there in stunned silence He suddenly disappeared. Where had He gone, what kind of individual is He, is He really a prophet? Is He as many have said the son of God?

Again, I didn't get to talk with Him since I didn't know it was Jesus, why hadn't I recognized him? I had to find out more about Him but in my heart, I knew He understood me and somehow my life would forever be changed. We were simply overjoyed and also in a state of shock, what did all of this mean? Why did this happen? Where had He disappeared to and why?

With Levi hurriedly now far ahead of us to deliver the goods to Uri, there was only myself and Cleopas left on the road to Nain. What indeed does the crucifixion mean, what is its impact on humanity? And where did Jesus go so suddenly disappearing after we recognized who the stranger really was? I had so many questions as we stood there in shocked silence.

CHAPTER SEVEN:

THE IMAPCT OF CHRISTIANITY

Where does one start to discuss the impact of Christianity and what Jesus' life and sacrifice did for humanity? Perhaps the best place to begin is to examine how it has changed the newly founded Thirteen Colonies as our country began to emerge. Our founding fathers knew they had to do something as they grappled with the founding of a new country, trying to ensure the pressures of the dictatorial states they left in Europe did not become a part of the newly founded American colonies. Many of our founding fathers were devoted Christians such as George Washington and Thomas Jefferson. Christianity had an enormous influence on how they set about to structure our nation. They concentrated on several freedoms, one freedom still vital today is the freedom of speech we all cherish and want to continue into our future despite the many pressures and persecutions in our modern society.

With a little research one can find out quickly that Christianity has led to the development of hospitals, food banks, homeless shelters, and many other various community outreach programs. These impactful programs can all be basically traced back to Christianity through the efforts of a community's local churches.

The impact of Christianity is mirrored everywhere in U.S. history. Examples of great Christian influences can be found reading about Martin Luther King Jr., William Wilberforce, and Mother Teresa to name only a few outstanding U.S. citizens found in our history.

When studying our history, the United States Constitution is one of the best examples of Christian influences that needs to be closely examined. This key document protects the many Christian beliefs that are so foundational to how our country has developed. Our citizens are free to participate in public and private worship of their choosing and protects our freedom to associate with other like-minded believers without any undue governmental interference and attend any church of choice. All Christians must cherish this right and fight to preserve all aspects of our Constitution in our current fast changing and often turbulent modern society.

A key question to consider, *"are we stepping out into our communities as Christians being visible examples helping to shape our local towns and cities showing compassion and love to insure there is a positive impact to all who come into contact with us as Christians?"*

We must guard against taking for granted our precious Christian foundational principals. Our values are indeed integral community attitudes and beliefs that make our nation great. All Christians can and should work at being a constant daily positive impact in our communities.

This little book is about being Christian but also is a small help for protecting all citizens and residents no matter what religion they have chosen.

The right to freedom of religion is really central to our American democracy and was firmly established in the First Amendment to the U.S. Constitution. The Founding Fathers wrote the First Amendment in response to religious persecution in Europe that often resulted from official state religions and religious wars.

Our Founding Fathers wisely put religion on a different footing from other forms of speech and observance. *They mandated strict separation of religion and government to ensure religious freedom for all individuals no matter what their faith was.* When studying our history, the First Amendment's prohibition against government regulation or endorsement of religion no matter the diverse faiths has become a part of America since the founding of the republic.

James Madison, our nation's fourth president, often called the "Father of the Constitution," said of the First Amendment as it relates to religion:

"It was the belief of all sects at one time that the establishment of Religion by law, was right and necessary; that the true religion ought to be established in exclusion of every other; And that the only question to be decided was which was the true religion. The example of Holland proved that the toleration of sects, dissenting from the established sect, was safe and even useful. The example of the Colonies, now States, which rejected religious establishments altogether, proved that all Sects might be safely and advantageously put on a footing of equal and entire freedom. We are teaching the world the great truth that governments do better without Kings and Nobles than with them. The merit will be doubled by the other lesson that Religion flourishes in greater purity, without than with the aid of Government." (Letter to Edward Livingston, July 10, 1822).

CONCLUSION

As we have tried to show in this little novella, Christianity has had a major influence in our nation and world from Biblical times to the present. *We should not and must not take for granted these Christian foundational principles will always endure.* As a Christian one needs to constantly step forward to make sure those, we come into contact with whether practicing Christians or not will understand the critical importance of our Christian values and beliefs are to the United States as well as to the entire world. All Christians must work together to ensure all people recognize the impact and value Christians have made to make our nation great.

Our founding fathers were so insightful building into our system of government "checks and balances' to protect our still developing system and process of democratic governing in this republic of ours.

How we live, work, and interact with others should always show and demonstrate the importance of our Christian beliefs and values.

ABOUT THE AUTHOR

**Prescott Chamber of Commerce Ambassador
ROBERT D. SHANKS JR.**

Prescott Chamber of Commerce Ambassador Bob Shanks served 31 years in the USAF starting out as an enlisted photo journalist. After his commissioning he then served as an intelligence analyst. He is also a certified instructor having taught English, journalism and special education before returning to the USAF full time. His last Air Force assignment was as a professor at the US Air Force Air War College, Maxwell AFB, AL.

Colonel Shanks began his military service as an enlisted photojournalist and engineering photographer. After four years of active duty, he returned to civilian life. He received his BA,

MS and PhD degrees from the University of Nebraska. During his college years he was an active member of the USAF reserve component serving as a reserve intelligence analyst working both for federal law enforcement as part of the war on drugs and the reserve. He served in seven major commands before joining the Air War College faculty. Bob served as an adjunct professor at Embry-Riddle Aeronautical University for ten years before totally retiring.

www.ingramcontent.com/pod-product-compliance
Lightning Source LLC
Chambersburg PA
CBHW071913070526
44583CB00016B/1973